MW01484421

# BUBA'S STORIES

# BUBA'S STORIES

*Beatrice Ruth Cohen Rossen*

iUniverse, Inc.
New York  Lincoln  Shanghai

# BUBA'S STORIES

Copyright © 2006 by Arlene Rossen Cardozo

All rights reserved. No part of this book may be used or reproduced by any means, graphic, electronic, or mechanical, including photocopying, recording, taping or by any information storage retrieval system without the written permission of the publisher except in the case of brief quotations embodied in critical articles and reviews.

iUniverse books may be ordered through booksellers or by contacting:

iUniverse
2021 Pine Lake Road, Suite 100
Lincoln, NE 68512
www.iuniverse.com
1-800-Authors (1-800-288-4677)

ISBN-13: 978-0-595-40671-5 (pbk)
ISBN-13: 978-0-595-85035-8 (ebk)
ISBN-10: 0-595-40671-8 (pbk)
ISBN-10: 0-595-85035-9 (ebk)

Printed in the United States of America

For Joseph and Lerah

# CONTENTS

## SECTION III: OUR HOMES

# *FOREWORD*

Beatrice Ruth Cohen Rossen, was Mother to my younger sister Ricky (Fredrica) Weiss and me, and Buba to her five grandchildren. From these stories of her Witebsky Cohen family, we get more than an inkling of the independent spirit which guided her throughout her 86 years and which caused this sophisticated well traveled woman who entertained governors and world medical leaders to announce when her first grandchild was born, "I will be called Buba".

My mother dictated these stories, which she had told us at various times over the years, within a six week period in the spring of 1997, and they are all in her voice. However she always referred to her grandparents Adolph and Fredrica Witebsky as Grandma and Grandpa, and to her parents Henry and Mary Cohen as Mama and Papa, but in transcribing I used their first names when she relates stories of their early years from before she was born. This signals the reader when she is relating what she heard them tell her about their pasts, as distinct from what she actually recalled from her own observations.

She stopped dictating over the summer, but I had hoped when winter came she would resume again with more Rossen history including the World War II years when my father enlisted in the Navy, his years as Minnesota's first Mental Health Commissioner, and the more than two decades she lived after his death as a dedicated Jewish community participant, Buba and single world traveler. However, Mother died in October 1997 before dictating any more stories, leaving us this priceless family history to which each of us can add histories of our own family continuations.

Arlene Rossen Cardozo

# SECTION I

# GRANDMA FREDRICA AND GRANDPA ADOLPH

# 1. A CHANCE MEETING

Grandma Fredrica and Grandpa Adolph used to look at each other and laugh when they told us grandchildren how they met.

"She backed right into me,"

Grandpa used to say.

"I don't have eyes in the back of my head," she'd retort.

They were not talking about a parking lot.

Fredrica Feitelson, petite darkhaired daughter of Riga mill owner Moshe Feitelson, was in the midst of an important lesson. She was in training to manage a household of which she would someday be mistress. As was usual in such circumstances, the family maid was showing her how to manage help by learning to do what she would then supervise her helpers doing. On that day the maid was teaching Fredrica to scrub the kitchen floor which had to be done on hands and knees. In order not to dirty a freshly scrubbed floor, Fredrica was learning to scrub her way out the back door, at the very moment that six-foot-two Adolph, young buyer trainee at the mill, came to deliver an important message to her father.

Startled by the impact, Adolph looked down and saw such a pretty young woman that he burst into laughter as he reached to help her up. "He was as tall as he was handsome," Grandma said, and from that moment none of the young Riga men considered suitable matches for Fredrica appealed to her. Adolph was highly capable and had learned the milling business quickly. And it was soon clear that she would marry him, though his station in life was dissimilar.

The bump on Grandpa's head came courtesy of his father— our great grandfather Samuel from the region of Vitebsk, when Adolph refused to pursue the occupation for which his father had planned since his birth.

"I'm going to be an astronomer, not a rabbi," Adolph maintained. When his father caught Adolph with the telescope he was told to discard, his father banged his head with it before throwing it away. Even when he grew old and bald, Grandpa would point to the still highly visable bump on his head and say, "And so that's why I left home."

"I followed the stars and went to seek my fortune as an astronomer. But I had to take what jobs I could get along the way until finally I arrived in Riga. Then, still in need of money to follow my dream, I took a job in the mill."

The Duke of Riga in the early 1880s, when young Adolph arrived, descended from a line of Dukes receptive to foreigners. Though there were many changes and boundary lines redrawn over the years, Fredrica's forebears came to Riga, likely through Germany from Spain after the Spanish Inquisition, imported in fact to help stimulate a lagging economy. By the 1880s at the time Adolph arrived, the Feitelsons were well integrated into Riga society, accepted and respected as mill (Fredrica's father) and department store (her uncles) owners.

However, by the time of Fredrica's marriage to Adolph, and the birth of four children—(one already deceased)—in the late 1880s, a new Duke arrived, whose cruel edict was unexpected and immediate.

All foreigners—meaning those not born within Riga—were to be exported within 48 hours, in order to create more work for Riga's citizens.

There was no way to pretend that Adolph was a native of Riga. He had arrived less than a decade earlier, a man from a locale so provincial that he bore no last name. When he married Fredrica he took the name Witebsky since he was from Vitebsk. He was doing well in the mill, but nonetheless it was widely known that he was not born in Riga.

A quick family council meeting was held. Overnight, Fredrica and Adolph's future, once so secure, and their expectations—to stay in Riga, he in the family business, she in their big, comfortable home raising their children, with the uncles, aunts and cousins around the corner—were shattered.

What to do? They would send Adolph to America. Fredrica and the children would follow, once he was established.

Adolph was sent by boxcar across the border. Fredrica's brothers hurriedly secured steerage passage and got Adolph and a small valise onto the next boat. Fredrica and their children would follow when he had an income and place for them to stay.

Adolph boarded in one of the "houses for men" established by Jews who had preceded him to New York. Like many other new immigrants he took what work he could find. In his case, selling straw chair backs on the street, at five cents apiece, of which he kept only a penny each.

Perhaps in a few months, or a year or two, like so many of his counterparts, he could have sent for Fredrica to join him in a lower east side tenement. But, when her brothers realized that Adolph had left their sister pregnant, they decided she should join him well before the birth of the new baby. And so it was that Fredrica, five-year-old Amelia, three-year-old Lena and tiny 18-month-old Mary, complete with samovar, candlesticks, silver, mirror and brush departed Riga in a stateroom: in her pocket was enough money pay a few months rent in New York.

Penny chair backs did not add up to much and by the time the new baby, Max, was a few months old, it was clear that the young father needed to seek other employment.

The same spirit of adventure and determination that once took him from Vitebsk to Riga, that saw him through his first months alone in New York, now enabled him to pack up his family, board a train with them and head to Minnesota. There, he heard from friends in New York, he would find thriving milling businesses; there he would once again do the gentleman's work for which he was well trained and highly experienced.

Adolph and Fredrica Witebsky—circa: mid-1890s

# 2. THE JEW PEDDLER

Adolph's hopes were dashed within days of his arrival in Minnesota. Jews were not allowed in milling. Thus, he had to join other Jewish immigrant men in earning a living on the road as a traveling salesman. But the mode of travel was not automobile and the term traveling salesman had yet to come. Adolph rented a horse and cart and became a peddler. As such he performed an important service for farm families too far from the Twin Cities, or even from smaller towns, to shop. A horse and buggy ride for them might take from one day to several; they had farms to tend and couldn't make pilgrimages to shop for necessary items, such as cloth, buttons (zippers were yet to be invented), thread, yarn for the farmwife to knit socks for her family, knitting needles, darning eggs to mend the socks (a wooden egg shape with a handle on it which a woman would deftly put in the stocking and darn around the hole), embroidery hoops, pins, work gloves, pants and shirts for the men, and family medicines such as peroxide. Thus the shop came to them!

Like the other peddlers, he did not own his wagon but rented it. He could speak German and did so with the German farmers while learning English from them. Always outgoing and jovial he quickly became popular with many farm families who often invited him to stay the night, and to eat with them. Unlike some of his counterparts who kept strictly kosher and did not accept such hospitality, Adolph, who had refused to become his father's "son the Rabbi," didn't believe in kashrut. That was for another time and place where the pottery was made differently, he said. It was "not for the modern world," he used to tell me. He also rejected a lot of other things that went along with strict Orthodoxy, while preferring to watch the stars!

Fascinated by the vast horizons where farmland merged with sky, he loved watching the heavens on clear nights, and shared these sights with his hosts' children. When he saw the Big Dipper or the Dog Star he'd rouse the children from their sleep and take them to watch with him. Stirred by his interest, they often become lifelong stargazing enthusiasts as a result of their midnight adventures with the man they fondly referred to as "the Jew Peddler."

Fredrica waited for Adolph to return with food or money; sometimes it was both. Some families paid in cash, others in fresh farm produce such as tomatoes, potatoes, cucumbers for pickling, and onions.

# 3. A STORE OF HIS OWN

Time passed. Adolph and Fredrica spent frugally and finally he was able to leave the horse and cart days behind and open his men's clothing shop in Bridge Square in Minneapolis, so named because it was located in the busy business section where the bridge over the Mississippi River intersected with Hennepin and Nicolett avenues. While his clientele came from all over the Twin Cities and surrounding areas, he specialized in lumbermen's clothes. Thus the store was filled with strapping men going off to the north woods in the spring in newly acquired clothes, and almost as full when they returned in the fall, with wages with which to pay for them. It was then that one man would reclaim his watch, another his candlesticks, yet another a ring that he had left as collateral, until returning with the means to pay for the clothes he'd worn all summer.

Some of the farm children to whom Adolph had once introduced the world of astronomy remembered him so fondly that they did their trading at his store when they came to the city. Now grown and owners of their own farms, they brought their children to meet him too. And they sometimes paid with their fresh produce as their fathers did before them. Only they brought it in bushel baskets on their trucks.

I can remember being at Grandma and Grandpa's big house on 6th Avenue when one of the trucks pulled up. The farmer came with many, many barrels; I counted five of them, but then I only could count to five, though I can picture more. They unloaded the bushels of carrots, parsnips, turnips, cucumbers, apples, potatoes and onions into Grandpa's winter shed. He was certainly not the only merchant paid this way. I remember Pete and Harold Levander (later a Governor of Minnesota) recalling going down into their cellar on Saturdays and "eyeing the potatoes," paid to their father. Many potatoes were stored there that had sprouted.

# 4. GRANDPA'S PICKLE BARREL

Grandma made wonderful soups and stews with most of the vegetables Grandpa was given by the farmers. But the cucumbers were reserved for Grandpa, who not only made the pickles but with great satisfaction considered himself quite the pickle maker. Proud of his black pickle barrel, he kept it full. Enlisting the older children to scrub the cucumbers until they gleamed, he also had them scrub and peel the carrots—only lengthways—for his prize recipe. He alone peeled the onions and his eyes never teared. When the vegetables were prepared he layered them in the barrel…each layer consisted of lots of cucumbers, then onion, and about half as many carrot slices as cucumbers.

He salted each layer. How much salt? A little sprinkled in his big hand for each layer. When the ritual was completed he placed a large plate upside down on top of the barrel, with a stone on top of his "pickle plate" to secure it, covered it all with a cloth and mandated at least a ten day wait until his recipe was fully pickled.

# 5. TRAGEDY

While Grandpa was building his clientele in the store, Grandma was steadily building the family on the home front. Four more daughters, in addition to Amelia, Lena, and Mary were born: Minnie (also the name of the baby who had died in Europe), Lucille, Rose and Evie—and another wonderful son. Then tragedy struck.

When that son was eight he developed a bad stomach ache. The doctor came immediately and looked grave. It was almost certainly appendicitis. The doctor rushed him to the hospital for surgery where he died of a ruptured appendix before surgery could be done. Fredrica and Adolph were shattered; the more so when, two days later, Fredrica gave premature birth to their last child, a son who arrived stillborn.

When Adolph went to the Minneapolis Jewish Cemetery to arrange to bury their sons he was told he had to pay immediately before the burial. With not enough cash, and unable to pay the bill with apples, potatoes or pawned watches, he was angry. Why was there nowhere a Jew could bury a loved one without the money? Why not somewhere totally free? Or at least where the bereaved could pay what they could? Or could pay what they could at the time and more later? Determined, Adolph proceeded to City Hall, got a long term lease on land adjacent to the present cemetery for a dollar—less than the burial cost at the existing cemetery—went home, got the bodies of his two sons and buried them. This was the beginning of the United Hebrew Brotherhood Cemetery in the Twin Cities.

# 6. SHABBOS GOY

The seven Witebsky girls and their brother grew. It was a merry home at 595 Sixth Avenue North with the children and their friends running in and out; and Fredrica baking batches and batches of her famous sugar cookies for them all. Because Mary and Max were less than two years apart, they shared many friends. Among them was Floyd B. Olson, who needed to help his family make ends meet. He asked Max to find out from his parents if he, Floyd, could become their "Shabbos Goy." Fredrica and Adolph liked the young lad and were quick to agree.

So every Shabbos the boy who would one day become Governor of Minnesota, and for whom 6th Avenue North would be renamed Olson Highway, lit the Witebsky furnace. If Max, who ordinarily shoveled the walk, was lucky enough for it to snow on Shabbos, Floyd shoveled the snow as well.

# 7. ADOLPH ORGANIZES
# THE SHUL

As the years passed Grandpa became more and more a pillar of the northside Jewish community. There was no synagogue when he arrived except for Reform Jews. So more observant Jews had their daily Minions, Shabbos and holiday services within one or another's homes.

Finally Grandpa convinced the others that if they all pooled their resources they could have a small synagogue space and they converted an old blacksmith shop, for which they paid fifty dollars, for that purpose.

This eventually became the core congregation of the lovely synagogue down the hill and around the corner from Grandma and Grandpa's house. On Lyndale and 6th Avenue North, it had beautiful stained glass windows and lots and lots of steps: steps up to the front door, and then more steps to the balcony where the women sat.

By the time I was born, over twenty years after Grandpa's arrival in Minneapolis, Grandpa had long been a Board Member of the Synagogue. He looked so fine and stately sitting there on the bimah facing the congregation: six foot two inches tall, huge dark eyes, handlebar mustache and tall silk hat. He was frequently sought to address community events because of his excellent and persuasive oratorical skills.

Below: Grandpa Adolph Witebsky and grandson Melvin Cohen, son of Mary Witebksy Cohen and Henry B. Cohen—circa: 1922

# SECTION II

# MARY AND HENRY AND BEATRICE RUTH

1. Mary

2. Henry

3. Beatrice Ruth

# 1. MARY

With Amelia already married to Abe Deutsch and Lena to Abe Rothstein, my beautiful mother Mary with the huge dark eyes and long dark hair was next in line.

She was in no hurry. Having left school, as did her older sisters, after 8th grade to help support the family, she first worked as a salesclerk in downtown Minneapolis' Donaldson's basement housewares department (Dayton's didn't hire Jews). She then moved up Nicollet Avenue to the fancier Maurice L. Rothchild store, where by age 21 she was assistant buyer in the boys department. She impressed Maurice L. early on with her quick mind, attention to detail, and sense of what would sell, in spite of—or perhaps because of—their first meeting.

She was up on a high ladder putting the finishing touches on a display when a man standing beneath called up, "Little girl, be careful up there, get yourself right down."

"Mind your own business," she shot back, not recognizing that the recipient of her insult was in fact MLR himself. When, a couple of years later, she told him she was leaving to marry Henry B. Cohen, he tried to keep her, and to hire Henry in the bargain. Even a service for 12 of Limoges china as a wedding present did not convince the young couple: Henry loved his independence, was doing well and was not about to work for someone else. And once a married woman Mary, of course, would not work for pay outside their home.

As a young working girl she lived at home, as girls did until they married, took the streetcar to work in bad weather and biked—as many girls did not—when it was clement. Weekend evenings were spent at house parties with other young single friends, male and female. Sometimes her crowd met at the Witebsky home and were joined by Max and some of her younger sisters. Other times they got together elsewhere.

Mary spent many Sundays at weddings. Known for her beautiful singing voice and marvelous piano playing, she was much in demand to add music to happy, festive celebrations. But Sunday August 21, 1910, was different. She was not rehearsing songs, nor was she at the keyboard. Mary was about to walk down the aisle to join Henry Benjamin Cohen in matrimony. If only the dress would go on smoothly. Amelia and Lena helped to pull the yards and yards of white satin over Mary's high pompadour, and then began buttoning the dozens of covered buttons of her brocade bodice. It fit easily over Mary's eighteen inch waist, enhanced her ample bosom, and looked glorious.

"It was the hottest day of the whole summer, and we were afraid the washtubs filled with chicken would spoil before the wedding feast," Grandma Fredrica used to tell us about our parents' wedding day.

Though the heat was overwhelming in Kissler Hall, more than 150 friends and relatives happily chatted, sought their seats and quieted down for the service. Adolph proudly escorted radiant Mary down the aisle to join Henry already standing at the Chuppah.

Below: Wedding portrait: Henry B. Cohen and Mary Witebsky Cohen, August 1910

# 2. HENRY

While Adolph then sat down with Fredrica and the large Witebsky clan in the front row, Henry had only his two brothers there. His brothers, Joe, who made the trip from Winnipeg to be with him, and Phil, who lived in Minneapolis, were holding two corners of the Chuppah. Max held another corner. Responsible for the match, he had met Henry the previous year, thought him a good prospect for Mary, and brought the near thirty-year-old bachelor home for dinner.

Already in Minneapolis for over ten years, Henry had left the farm of his father Isaac outside of Telz, Lithuania, for America at his father's insistence. Two older brothers had been taken into the Army years before, one gone a decade, the other never to return. Determined that this fate not befall his other sons, his father provided Joe, Phil and Henry (as each came of age for military service) with enough hard earned money to get to, and get started in, the new world.

Well educated by yeshiva students (from the famed Telz yeshiva) who stayed with them each summer and taught the boys, Henry was ready when his turn came. He was sad to leave his father and his home. His mother, Basha, was long gone, having been accidentially hit on the head by a brick from the stove when he was only two.

Two stepmothers, the first far worse than the second, followed. In fact, Papa used to tell us that his little stepsister from his fathers first marriage after the death of his mother, saved his life. The stepmother conserved money by not feeding her husbands growing sons. However, there was always food for her baby daughter, Mary. The little girl loved her older brothers, though, and often saved her food for them.

Finally the older boys had their chance to retaliate against their stepmother in spades. The wicked stepmother was in hard labor with her second daughter. Their father sent them to get the doctor. They took their time and by the time the doctor arrived their stepmother was dead. The boys took the credit.

When Henry arrived in America he went right to Minneapolis where Phil was already established as owner of the only Jewish bakery between Chicago and Denver. He worked for Phil, while he learned the language at night school. Then he began peddling menswear, happy to be back in farmland again.

Within a couple of years, Henry saved what he needed, added to the money which his father had sent him, and opened Security Clothing on Hennepin Avenue in the Bridge Square area. Upstairs of the store was the St. James Hotel. The clientele was primarily transient men newly arrived, in search of work, or merely passing through the area.

By the time Henry began courting Mary he was in position to propose marriage soon. And Mary having met someone with similar intelligence and interests in building the Jewish community of Minneapolis, was ready.

# 3. BEATRICE RUTH

There wasn't much time for the newlyweds to get acquainted as a married couple because it was nine months until I arrived on the scene, a month early much to my mother's embarrassment. "It's a good thing I had one period after I was married," she used to say, "or people would have talked." (But how would they have known she had a period I always wondered.)

The legendary Dr. George Gordon took my mother in his horse and buggy, as he always did when a patient went into labor, to the hospital. He delivered me and a few hours later was back in the neighborhood to get Aunt Amelia and then he delivered my birthday twin cousin Chuckie. We were born on May 30 which then was Memorial Day. It always rained on our birthday; I wonder if it always rained for Memorial Day before we were born, too.

I was born at Asbury Hospital. Both Asbury and St. Mary's took Jews at the time, but most Jews didn't like to go to St. Mary's because of all the crucifixes around. Jews were excluded from certain hospitals far into the 1950s. When I was pregnant in 1941 with Ricky, Kay (wife of Harold who used to work under Daddy) used to always throw it up to me: "Abbott is the best hospital; too bad you can't go there where I'm going to have my baby."

I was named Beatrice, for Papa's mother who was Basha, but Ruth was for no one in the family; it was because it was Mama's favorite name. Nobody at home, or in the extended family, ever called me Beatrice anyway; it was always Ruthie.

Finally when Mama took me to register at Lincoln School (later called John Hay School because John Hay was Abe Lincoln's Secretary of State; when the Junior High was built it got Lincoln's name and the grade school became John Hay School), the secretary in the Principal's office asked, "What is your name?"

"Beatrice Cohen," I said before Mama could say Ruth. I was five and a half then and I got to be Beatrice at school.

# SECTION III

# OUR HOMES

# Our Homes

We lived in three houses while I was growing up and, of course, we spent lots of time at my grandparents' home on Sixth Avenue North.

The house Mama and Papa first lived in was a duplex on Highland Avenue, three blocks from my grandparents and next door to Uncle Phil and his family. That was my first home.

Next, we moved to 1134 James Avenue when I was about two. It was meant to be a temporary house, but we lived there for four and a half years because of the War (WWI). Ethel was born during the time we lived there.

Then we moved to 1241 Upton Avenue North in April, 1918, three months after Mel was born. (This is the home that ultimately five generations of Witebsky descendants lived in: Grandpa Witebsky, after Grandma died, lived there with all of us; my folks (Henry and Mary) raised Ethel, Mel and me there, and my Aunt Lucy lived with us some of the time; then Ralph, Arlene, Ricky and me, and my father after his stroke; then the grandchildren—Miriam, Rachel, Rebecca and Ben—all but Ralee spent overnights in that house.)

I have vivid recollections of each of these homes.

# 1. MY GRANDPARENTS' HOME

## Chamberpot

An early, early memory is of the chamberpot in the bedroom of my grandparents' house; I think they had a bathroom by then but they still kept the pot, maybe in case the bathroom was busy; I don't know. It was a wooden frame chair with a hole in the bottom and then a cover went over the hole. It was all white with pink flowers.

## Telephone

I still remember my grandparents' telephone number. It was Hyland 1565, but at first the number was just 1565 without the Hyland prefix. Ours on Upton was Hyland 1570.

# Holidays

Holidays with my grandparents were wonderful. Their dining room table expanded to become big, bigger and bigger. All of us cousins—twenty of us used to get to sit at the table with Grandma and Grandpa and our fathers. Our mothers loved to sit on the radiator cover in the big bay window and eat on their laps just like they did when they were growing up. My sister and I got to stay overnight when we were young, as did two of our other cousins. We lived too far to walk both ways, so our parents walked over with us and then they walked home at night, carrying our little brother.

Then, after everyone left, Grandpa would pull out the big living room couch into a bed and all four of us would get into bed and talk and laugh ourselves to sleep. During the day we would go to the synagogue to visit the grownups. We had to be careful not to run in and out during certain prayers but otherwise we went to visit our Grandpa and our fathers downstairs and then upstairs to the balcony to visit Grandma and our mothers. There was a big playground in the back and we played out there while we waited for the grownups to be done.

We especially liked Yom Kippur because, as on Rosh Hashanah, we would wear our new holiday dresses and, besides that, Grandma would dress all in white. It was nice to see her so dressed up because, except for the holidays, we rarely saw her without her freshly washed, ironed and starched apron on. And, as she always did when we were with her, she would hug and kiss us and if it needed it brush our hair with her big silver brush.

There was always lots of good food to eat at Grandmas but especially on the holidays. Other days she always had the soup kettle going. This was no ordinary kettle but rather a huge black iron pot and it seemed always to be on the stove although I'm sure they put it in the summer kitchen overnight. She would put every possible vegetable in, and then add to it constantly. If there was a little meat leftover from one meal, some chicken from another, she'd cut it up and put it in. If it cooked too far down, she'd add water; if there was too much broth she'd add more vegetables or meat and so it went.

One thing I can clearly remember was the desserts, the platters of great big cookies and Grandma Fredrica asking Mel, when he was maybe one or two, "Have a cookelah, Moshe?"

Below: The Witebsky home at 595 Sixth Avenue North, Minnespolis.

## The Witebsky Clan

The Witebsky clan was a solid unit; we didn't really need anybody else. My cousin Chester and I were born just a couple of hours apart; my cousin Jeanette and I were very close too. There were almost twenty of us: Aunt Amelia had Adeline, Frank, Chester, Dolly and Devorah; Aunt Lena had Edith, Ceil, Helen, Harriet, Jeanette and the four boys; then there was the three of us; Uncle Max moved to California and had just Bennett so we never saw him; and Aunt Minnie had Bobbie and Fritzi. Aunt Lucy never married, Aunt Rose never had children either, and Aunt Evie along with Aunt Rose moved to Chicago and married. Later Evie adopted her husband's two children, but we didn't really know them either.

Our unit was of the four sisters, Amelia, Minnie, Lena and Mama who between them had 18 children. On Sundays we'd go on picnics together and there were birthday parties and holidays, and we saw each other at school. That's why later it was so lonesome; by after the war almost everybody moved away.

# 2. HIGHLAND AVENUE

My recollections of the outside of our house would be vague except that throughout my life I drove past it as my shortcut from Upton Avenue to downtown Minneapolis. It was high on a hill above where the Farmers Market is now, near my grandparents—three blocks away in fact—near Oak Lake in which Grandma Fredrica would never let us swim because she felt it wasn't clean. (Years later, the first Talmud Torah on Fremont Avenue had an indoor swimming pool, but my Mother didn't let us swim there because the janitors didn't change the water except when they decided to.)

I have three distinct recollections of events in my life while we were living on Highland: cucumbers, noodles and a china doll.

## Cucumbers

Mama had guests for lunch and she fixed lovely salad plates for each of them. Then she put the plates out at each place just before the guests were to arrive. Then she went back into the kitchen. Then I went to the table and I scientifically went around to each place and I ate all the cucumbers from each plate. I'm sure I got sick and threw up afterwards.

## Noodles on the Grill

When I was little—I couldn't have been over two years old—you couldn't buy noodles in the store, you had to make them yourself. We had a grill (grate) on the floor; the furnace was way underneath and then forced air would come up through the grill. Mama put papers over the grill—I recall writing on them but I don't think she would have used newspapers—and then after she cooked the noodles on the stove, she would place them there to dry. I saw her from across the room and I got over to the grill and made a hole in the papers and then pushed each noodle through until I got rid of them all.

## My China Doll

One Hanukah when I couldn't have been over three I was given a beautiful china doll with a gorgeous head and face—all china. I'd never seen such a wonderful doll because I'd always had rag dolls before. I could hardly wait until the next morning when I could show my new doll my very favorite toy of all, my toy rockinghorse. When I introduced my doll to my rockinghorse, I let her go on him and rock. After that it was back to rag dolls!

# 3. JAMES AVENUE

Papa sold the duplex when I was about three, shortly after Ethel was born, as he had purchased adjacent lots on Girard and Humboldt Avenues North on which to have a home built. We rented 1134 James avenue North supposedly for a short time while they were building, but then the war broke out (WWI) and it was not possible for them to go on with their plans. Materials were in terribly short supply and builders were most all in the service.

So the short term rental lasted for four years, during which we lived in our temporary yellow house with the gas lamps outside. There were two very exciting happenings there: the lamplighter, and the picture man.

## The Lamplighter

I could hardly wait until dark when the lamplighter would come and light each lamp. I'd sit in the window and watch—we were not allowed outside after dark—and I thought what he was doing to make those lights go on was just wonderful. He came every night as it started to darken, and hoisted his lighted long pipe up to the street light (one was directly in front of our living room window). He lit the gas in the fixture and walked on to the next one. I couldn't wait until he would come at night, and kept my face pressed against the windows to watch him. These were not our lamps, they were the street lamps.

## The Picture Man

The picture man came with a cart and a goat. We sat in the cart and had "professional" pictures taken with the goat. Mama had a camera, and took loads of pictures of us, but the goat cart was different!

Above: Ethel and I in the goat cart for our "professional picture."

## Water for Papa

On James we had a small park close to the house. We would walk up a little hill to get there; every late afternoon before Papa came home Ethel and I would walk up there to the pump which had fine water; we would fill a jug with fresh water for Papa's dinner.

## Transportation

When we lived on Highland we had no car. Papa rented carriages as he needed them, larger or smaller depending upon the need for it, but he owned his horse which was kept in a stable a few blocks from home. I don't remember if we had a car when we lived on James or not, but we sure did on Upton.

## Roller Skating

My very most enduring memory of those years on James Avenue is rollerskating—that street is where I first learned, and that is where I used to race with Arnie Grais (later the pharmacist) down James Avenue until I generally ended up in the alley driveway on my knees in the cinders. My knees were most always skinned from those wonderful times but at least it was safe in that very few people had cars then. I continued rollerskating after we moved but it wasn't ever the same without Arnie to race with; however, my knees looked better after that.

One additional memory that I have is that while we stayed on James Avenue, Papa let people who lived near our two lots (the ones on which we were planning on building a home after the war) plant victory gardens on the land.

## Clothes

When we lived on James, and also later on Upton, the Sewing Lady came twice a year to measure us and make our clothes. Mama made some of them, too. She made our Mary Mixup Dresses. They were made of taffeta with great big bows in the back. They were quite the rage.

# 4. UPTON AVENUE

Though Papa had planned to build us a house, and he owned those two lots on which to do it, after World War One was over, the house on the corner of Upton and Plymouth Avenues in Homewood became available. Jews were allowed there, and so we moved there. Billy Porter's father (Billy was in my room at school) and mother had planned the house, but then Billy's mother died before they could move in and his father married her nurse. The nurse didn't want to live in the house that his first wife had planned.

Homewood allowed Jews and so Papa and Mama decided it was silly to build as they loved the Upton Avenue house. However, Grandma Fredrica was afraid of us living there because of all the woods behind us where you could hear the wolves howling at night.

Mel was born just before we moved in (he on January 16, 1918, the house in April) and I remember Papa telling us that we had a little brother. When we moved in Mama got her beautiful Steinway, which she loved to play, and to sing while she played. She bought a less expensive dining room set so as to have the money for the piano.

Above: the Henry Cohen family home at 1241 Upton Avenue North, Minneapolis, in which 5 generations of the Witebsky/ Cohen/Rossen lived between its purchase in 1919 and its sale in 1973.

## Mel's Lice

Mel got lice from a little boy across the street; he had two neighbor friends Bobby Neigle and Billy Walker. He and Billy had changed caps one day and then Mel was itching and they sent him home after sending him to the nurse. Mama was so embarrassed; finally she and her sisters got him all cleaned and scrubbed up.

# Ethel's and My Adventures in the Fields

When Ethel and I were maybe four and seven, we would walk over a little footbridge which is where Ewalds kept their cows. (This is the area now known as Theodore Wirth Park). Sometimes we would go and talk to the tall man who used to walk there about his plans. He would take out pictures and tell us what he planned to do. He said he would "build a winding road so that people wouldn't go fast and could see the beauty." It turned out that he was Theodore Wirth. He had this idea, his dream. He wanted those flower gardens set aside, too (now Eloise Butler). Imagine little kids running around the whole neighborhood.

It was early spring and Ethel and I wanted to go and see if the "cowslips" (the marsh marigolds) were blooming. Mama said we could go but to stay on the bridge—a little wooden structure across Bassett's Creek. We looked from the bridge and saw ice on the water, so we decided to cross the ice. We were wearing boots up to our knees anyway. But we fell through the ice and got soaked up past our boots. We hurried home but we were scared to go in. We sat on the back steps and emptied our boots, which were filled with water. Mama was just shaking when she found us. She took us up and put us in a tub of hot water. She rubbed us down, shaking and scolding us all the while.

## Plows

They plowed the sidewalks not the streets. So people could walk. Early plows were just a wooden thing; a man sat on it and the horse pulled it. The streetcar had a special kind of plow so it could run but very few people had cars and even fewer used them in the winter. They took the wheels off and put them upon wooden "horses" (framed wooden things) and left them in the garages. Some people had something like a garage for their buggy. I don't recall any horses and buggies in Homewood. Papa got a Chandler when we moved up on Upton, with silver handles to open the doors and we would stand up. We thought it was wonderful!

# Grandma Mary's Driving

Papa taught Mama to drive. Soon afterward she piled Ethel and me into the backseat, put Mel in the front and drove us down Plymouth Avenue to Morgan to pick up Aunt Lena and cousin Jeannette. Aunt Lena lived down a hill. Mama couldn't remember which was the clutch and which was the brake, so we went very, very fast. Finally she stopped the car, Aunt Lena got in the front with her and held Mel; Jeanette got in back with us and off we went to the butcher shop. We didn't get there.

Mama got mixed up about the brake again and a telephone pole hit our car. Mama promptly got out, found a telephone and called Papa to report the errant pole. "A pole came right up and hit us," she told him. She didn't drive again for a longtime; usually we all went by streetcar.

## Downtown

On the weekends on Sundays we went to Sunday school. On Saturday afternoons we occasionally stayed home with the maid or played in the neighborhood but usually we went downtown. Papa went to shul on Saturday morning, napped in the afternoon, and then went to the store. While Papa was at the store Mama would drop us downtown while she did her errands. She would take us to the wonderful Orpheum or Pantages Theater, and we would watch moving pictures and vaudeville. Some of the vaudeville people went on to Broadway and we got to see them first for ten cents each.

After the show we would go over to Witts on Hennepin Avenue and buy a cake to bring home for dinner—but first we'd stand outside and watch the man make banana cream pies through the window. Other times we'd go to Johns and pick up some chow mein to bring home for dinner. (To be eaten on Mamas third set of dishes, she had the milk the meat and the Chinese.)

Mel recalls that when Ethel and I were older and no longer accompanying them, Grandma Mary and he went to a Saturday afternoon movie, then out to eat at John's (he does not remember the Chinese food at home) then back to a second movie while Papa finished at the store in the evening. He also remembers all the dishes at home (sans the Chinese) milk and meat for everyday, milk and meat for holidays and then milk and meat for Pesach as well.

# Hired Girls

Mama and Papa got many maids from one of the families fond of Papa who remembered a younger Henry from his peddling days. There were no suitors available for their many daughters in their small farm town, so one family sent each of their daughters, in turn, to live with us in exchange for room, board and a small allowance while they did housework, babysat and Papa searched among his non-Jewish clientele for suitable mates for them. Our maids in those day were called "hired girls" and that is what they called themselves as well.

All of Mama's friends had hired girls, too. That freed them to do important Jewish communal work. There were no meetings, though, on Thursday afternoons or Sundays; those times were maids' days off.

# My Grandparents…

Grandma Fredrica was always warm and loving to all of us. She used to go to the lake with us on Sundays when we had the first cars which were open at the sides like they all used to be. But once we got a closed car she wouldn't go anymore; she hated feeling closed in.

She never brought up having to leave Riga and everybody there, unless she did to Grandpa or her children but never to us or in front of us. She had more than the house and the children, she had her lady friends and they did work in the community. There was no burial society, so when there was a death, she and her friends tended the bodies until later they founded the burial society.

Grandma had diabetes, and died when I was about eleven. After that Grandpa came to live at our house. He was always such fun. All the time we were growing up he would take each grandchild to the fair, in turn, so each got a special day with him.

When I first remember Grandpa Adolph he was very tall......6 foot 1, was quite bald and had a white handlebar moustache. He looked so handsome and imposing up on the bimah.

Grandpa was a fabulous orator. He gave orations in Yiddish, too.

"Here I Witebsky," he'd say when he answered the phone.

He used to take each grandchild to the fair, taking turns so that he took only one at a time.

Even in later years when he had his store, he kept in contact with the farmers he once knew. So when he bought merchandise for the store he sometimes exchanged it for farm goods which used to be delivered to their home at 595 6th Avenue North. I remember the huge bushelbaskets being delivered, and remember counting up to five, which was as high as could count at the time. There were really a lot more apples, onions, cucumbers, and potatoes than anything else.

Grandpa lived for several years after Grandma died, and he lived at our house. I can remember his last birthday, his 71st. Mama and my aunts (the girls as he called them) made him a huge three layer cake, and he blew out every candle.

# SECTION IV

# MAMA AND PAPA BUILDING THE MINNEAPOLIS JEWISH COMMUNITY

When Mama and Papa drank from their joint cup at the altar they began their 39-year journey together during which they not only raised their family of three children, me—Beatrice Ruth (Basha Rifka for his mother)—Ethabelle (for Isaac, his deceased father) and Melvin Samuel (Moshe Samuel for her grandfathers), but helped found and build many Jewish community institutions.

There was the Oak Park Children's Home, originally called the Oak Park Jewish Sheltering Home for Children, which they began with Mrs. Farbstein because of the TB epidemic. Those afflicted with the disease needed to be out of the house, so as not to infect others, while they were cared for to recovery.

Papa was a founder of the Jewish Home for the Aged of the Midwest, located in St. Paul. Mr. Robicheck, a manufacturer and friend, helped him in this.

Both Mama and Papa were on the Board of the Talmud Torah. Mama and her friends founded Minneapolis' first Hadassah chapter.

When the doorbell rang once too often on a Sunday with yet another Jewish neighbor collecting for another good Jewish cause, Papa helped institute the Minneapolis branch of the Federation of Jewish Service so that donations to many institutions could be made with a single check.

Their work in founding the three organizations that I remember the most about were the Oak Park Sheltering Home for Children, Beth El Synagogue and Minneapolis Chapter of Hadassah.

# 1. OAK PARK SHELTERING HOME FOR CHILDREN

Mr. and Mrs. Farpstein lived upstairs of our duplex on Highland Avenue—we lived high on a hill over where the Farmers' Market is now—very near my grandparents. The Farpsteins had a son and daughter and another girl they took care of; before long Mrs. Farpstein had six children upstairs.

There was a lot of TB in the community; families were separated, the well parent had to earn a living and there were no facilities to take care of the children. So the Farpsteins were taking care of them, it seems.

Mr. Farpstein was a barber who had a shop downtown. The Farpstein's found this house on Elwood and were able to get it with my father's help. I think that at that time Jewish Family and Children's Service did nothing to help these children with TB and did not want any kind of home for them.

My father and the Farpsteins took the children in my father's horse and buggy to this home on Elwood, and from then on it become Oak Park Sheltering Home for Children.

# 2. BIRTH OF BETH EL

Mama and Papa were active in their Saturday night Club, a continuation really of the singles clubs to which Mama belonged earlier, in that now it was groups of couples who met in one another's homes. One night during a current events program someone reported on the newly forming Conservative Jewish movement.

Papa spoke emphatically that he feared that their American born Jewish children would be lost to Judaism if they were forced to choose either Orthodoxy—which many already rejected—or Reform Judaism, the only other alternative.

Recognizing the need for a middle ground he and Mama and some of their friends pooled resources and bought an old home at 14th and Penn Avenue North. The women quickly kashered the kitchen, baked and cooked and sponsored fundraising dinners and bake sales to help finance a real building. Grandpa and the men sought donations from all their Jewish business colleagues.

The Tremblatts, Cutts, Weinberg and Weinstien and many other families joined the effort. All were initially thrilled to have their own shul—albeit an old maroon house—but the moreso when construction on what was soon to be Beth El Synagogue began. As children, we used to walk by the old house, pinching ourselves and saying to each other, "That's our new shul, that's our new shul."

When our huge corner building with reception hall, red carpets and plush red seats, and stained glass windows was finally done, we danced until dawn. Papa stayed with his original shul as well, though, long after it became Kenneseth Israel, the most prominent of the Orthodox congregations. He himself was never very comfortable with the Conservative Service (even in the new Beth El he and his friends had their own Orthodox service in the basement where somehow magically even without a Shabbos goy they managed to prevent the Rabbi's sermon from being piped in.)

# 3. BIRTH OF THE MINNEAPOLIS CHAPTER OF HADASSAH

I remember when I was about seven years old, coming in from school when my mother and her girlfriends had their sewing club. Most were friends from grade school; they had played together as children, attended school together, gone to the same parties as young women. Many married men from the same grade school crowd. Now, as young mothers most lived in the same neighborhood as one another: Homewood, in North Minneapolis.

Their sewing club was much like a minyon. Somebody gave a book review or reported on an article at each meeting. They met one afternoon a week and brought whatever handiwork they had to do; sewing, mending, whatever it was.

One afternoon somebody reported on an article about Henrietta Szold and the work she was doing with maternal and child health in Palestine. The article mentioned the need for diapers and layettes for the children that were born in these clinics. The sewing club decided that they would try to help.

My father went to the wholesale house and bought flannel by the bolt; the women met every week, cut and hemmed the diapers and each week he would ship a box of what they made to the New York office that had been mentioned in the article.

In addition, on their own time outside the group, the women made sweaters, bonnets, booties, etc., which they brought to the weekly meetings and my father shipped them as well.

This group was the beginning of the Minneapolis chapter of Hadassah. Actually the same group of women plus their husbands started Beth El.

# SECTION V

# THE LAKES

1. Tonka Bay
2. Summers at the Lake
3. Worms

# 1. TONKA BAY

We went to Tonka Bay on Sundays, sometimes the grandparents went but usually we went with some of our aunts and uncles and cousins. Grandma Fredrica liked the open cars, those that first came out, but later when Papa got a Chandler which was all covered she didn't like to go anymore; she hated being closed in it. Ethel and I loved the Chandler with the bright silver handles; we could stand up in the backseat and look out. Grandma never brought up having to leave Riga and everybody there, unless she did to Grandpa or to her children but never to us or in front of us. She had more than the house and the children; she had her lady friends and they did work in the community.

# 2. SUMMERS AT THE LAKE

From the time we lived on James, or maybe even before, I had what they called "summer complaint," the symptoms of which I do not remember because it was apparently alleviated by the doctor's prescription: take her out of the city to the lake. Thus began our summers at Lake Minnetonka, first at Tonka Bay and later at Mound, both of which allowed Jews.

Mama would take me, (and as they were born Ethel and Mel) when school was out. We'd rent a cabin and Papa would come out after sundown Saturday and go back Sunday night. As the years went on the Deutsch family used to rent an adjacent cabin, and Mama would invite each of the Rothstein children who wanted to come for a two week vacation (I only remember the girls coming) so we were never alone there. In much later years when we girls felt too old to go with the family, a group of us would rent our own cabin for a week and stay at the lake. Throughout my growing years, I only remember that we missed one summer; the year when I was seven and got rheumatic fever. We'd just moved to Upton Avenue, and Dr. Neumann said the house was big and airy enough that it was best for me to stay in bed—which he made me do all summer—there rather than at the lake.

I loved so to dance, Mama said my feet never touched the ground when I was little, but Dr. Neumann said I shouldn't take dancing anymore. So my parents switched me to the violin. Mr. Kammens, the Minneapolis Symphony orchestra violinist who rented the upper part of my grandparents' big house, said I had the "stance of a violinist" and so I duly took lessons; but I never loved it like dancing.

Mrs. Kammens trained their yellow canary Caruso to sing and then she let Mama buy him, so Caruso sang in our sunroom at Upton.

# 3. WORMS

I can see Mama in the deep woods with Ethel and me out at
Minnetonka digging worms. Ethel and I wore tall black boots;
the woods were wet from the night before. We used to go and
stay at Mound some summers too. We rented from an Indian
man married to a Jewish woman. He owned the cabins, was an
alcoholic and sometimes went out in the boat and got
stupefied. Sometimes the neighbors would get him back
together and bring him in. The couple also rented out rooms to
teachers in the main building…teachers got room and board—
there was a restaurant, too. Later they built a mansion for
people who wanted a fancier vacation. He knew the places on
the lake where fishing was the best. Fish were pretty limited in
the lake. After Mama died, during shiva, Mel and I went out
there one afternoon to bring back memories.

As to digging worms, I must have been a little older when I
remember doing it because I put my own worms on the hook.
Ethel was probably 2 and a half or so and I was 4 or 5. It was
after the rain that we used to dig for the worms, because they
would come to the top. We wore boots so we wouldn't get our
feet wet. I hated putting the worms on—I hated it, OOOOf—
but not so much as I hated minnows.

Ethel and I used to go in the boat with Mama to fish, and then we'd come back to the cabin and watch her make fish soup for Papa for when he came out after Shabbos for Sundays with us. Also, we had water wings; we were being taught to swim.

Mama got her love for the country and the water from going out for the day on picnics with her family. Grandpa Witebsky would rent a horse and buggy and they'd go.

The big Minnetonka and Excelsior Hotels had signs out:

NO DOGS

NO JEWS

NO NIGGERS

When Floyd Olson became Governor he really went to town and cleaned up the state. He made them stop the stuff against the Jews; he had Jewish friends like Mama and Uncle Max, was a Shabbos goy, so he knew Jews. He did a lot that Humphrey got the credit for; he appointed Daddy, the first Jew to work in the state hospitals. (When Humphrey worked in the drugstore near the Medical School, and the Noble apartments, on Washington Avenue we used to call him "Pinky" because he was such a socialist.)

Well, back to the lake. The reason we stopped going to Tonka Bay was because there was a terrible wreckage from a huge electrical, hailstorm. I remember being on the front porch and the hail was terrible. It ruined the porch and the cottage, there was broken glass all over. We left after the storm; they had to rebuild the cottages.

# SECTION VI

# SCHOOLS

# 1. STARTING SCHOOL—JOHN HAY

It was from James Avenue that I first went to school. We were in the Grant district and Mama had a fit—she did not consider Grant a good school and she got me transferred to John Hay.

One day I was late. That morning, I walked to school which was about six blocks away, and I hid outside by the sidewalk behind some cement step or something. I was afraid to go in because I was late so I stayed in hiding until the teacher came to look for me. I had to stay after school for a week and then Mama lit into the teacher and they didn't make me stay after anymore.

# 2. ANTISEMITISM AT WILLARD

John Hay School was overcrowded and Lincoln hadn't been built yet. The neighborhood was divided; one side of the street was sent to John Hay, the other to Willard. I was sent to Willard in fourth grade. Nobody was nice to me because I was Jewish.

Two girls in the neighborhood who lived across Plymouth from us were nice to me sometimes. Charlotte and Lindall, whose father used to help with our yard and with shoveling our snow, walked to school with me sometimes. But only until they saw others going that direction. Then they took off and went with the others and let me walk alone, saying "Nice people weren't seen with Jews."

During recess I stood alone, leaning against the building, and ate the apple Mama packed for me, watching the other kids play and have fun.

There were two ball teams and naturally I was not invited to participate. That is until the year the Grodnicks moved to town from Dakota. One day, at outside gym their daughter, Genevieve, hit the baseball so hard that it sailed high across the school ground to the very end. She made a comfortable homerun while the others stood with their mouths open, not believing it. Jew or not, both teams had to have her, neither could afford not to. She told them in no uncertain terms that she couldn't play baseball unless I was also on the team. So we joined one of them and I became a fielder.

They lived on 14th and Sheridan, and we stayed friends over the years. Her parents desperately wanted me to marry her brother but of course I didn't. Genevieve moved back to Dakota, married a Sharp, and we stayed in touch and met for lunch when she visited here. She was one of my closest friends.

Oh, and there was the anti-Semitic principal, the bitch; she kept me after school; I didn't know why. One day I was supposed to meet Mama on Queen and Plymouth for dancing school. We were to get a certain streetcar at a certain time but of course I wasn't there. I was crying at school because they wouldn't let me go and meet Mama like I was supposed to. Then Mama came, found me and the principal, and told her off but good and got me out of there.

That principal and Dean Anne Dudley Blitz were so alike you would have thought they were sisters. I remember Dean Anne with the hat full of feathers coming up to me in Dayton's Tea Room…"I remember you, you're our charming little girl."

# 3. LESSONS

I was taking private dramatics lessons from about age nine—elocution lessons they were called—after the doctor made me stop dancing. Then my teacher, Hazel Lawrence, got married and I stopped elocution for a while. These were private lessons. Hazel rented studio space at MacPhail. Sometimes we wrote our dramatics pieces; sometimes 2 or 3 of us got together and performed.

When I moved over to Lincoln I was involved at the paper and considered an outstanding writer. I wrote a piece called "Mama and Papa Gym Classes" and from then on I was considered quite the writer. My parents went at night to the classes they had.

Papa married an American girl; he wanted the American way. Education, education, education—he didn't care what it was just so it was education.

We all had piano lessons. Mel was the best, Ethel was next best, and I was lousy.

Below: We Three—Melvin, Ethabelle and Beatrice Ruth Cohen at my confirmation in 1926

# 4. NORTH HIGH AND ABIE

On my first day at North High I opened my locker and heard a loud scream. It didn't come from within the locker but rather from the floor. I looked down to the source of the noise and saw a head full of brown curls. When the owner of them stood up and glowered down at me, I saw that I'd bashed his head with the locker door. When he saw how flustered I was he broke into a grin, introduced himself as Abie Berman and said we might as well get used to each other. We did.

We went together all through High School. He'd walk me home, carrying my books and then walk all the way back to his house, which was a mile and half from our house, close to school. Abie and I used to go for a malted milk for 15cents and two straws and an extra paper cup. At North High the meeting place was by the statue. Mr. Hobbes would stand there to chase us away. He didn't like loitering around the statue.

By the time we got to the U Mama insisted that I needed to go out with others, even though she liked Abie a lot. She felt I'd only ever gone with him and I needed to branch out. And there were so many around. So Abie used to sit near me, not with me, in the library and then when a fellow seemed interested, Abie would come over and make a fuss over me which would get the new person even more interested.

We sort of drifted apart and we talked about getting back together but it never happened. We were always very very good friends, and he used to come and visit after he moved to California where he practiced medicine, and lived with his wife and family.

His sister Vivian lives in the building (Knollwood), she was a social worker.

# 5. U OF M AND MCPHAIL

The fall after I graduated from North High, I began the University of Minnesota. We wore dresses and trekked all over the campus in our high heels. Dean Anne Dudley Blitz was Dean of Women. I hated her.

It seemed that they always had a way to spoil the classes that sounded like such fun, such as Astronomy. I liked to look through the big telescope at the stars and constellations, but mostly we had to study the text book, do boring work in class and take tests.

I pledged SDT, the Jewish women's sorority, but did not join. I had a fight with the sorority president, threw my pin at her, and left. They tried to tell me who I could date, and who I could be friendly with, and who I couldn't.

Instead, I belonged to an off-campus sorority of Jewish girls and had a lot of fun with them. Nobody told us who we could see.

Since elocution and acting was what I really loved and I could not get at the U nearly as well as I could at McPhail School of Dramatic Arts, I transferred there, and graduated from there. I was in plays, took elocution, and memorized a whole repertoire of dramatic readings. That meant I was able to teach dramatics, which I did. I gave private lessons.

# One of Life's Most Embarrassing Moments

I had graduated McPhail and my graduation piece was considered very good. So I was invited by the auxiliary of the Oak Park Children's Home to do a program for a meeting. It was a lovely building with a landing and tall winding staircase. I did my reading and then there was applause and I looked at the crowd and I saw that some people seemed to be looking at me in wonderment. So instead of pausing and bowing and accepting their applause as I'd been taught, and always done at McPhail, I turned and bolted up the stairs. Don't ask me why.

Afterwards Mama asked, "Now why did you do that?" and I said I wished I knew.

# SECTION VII

# BEA AND RALPH

# 1. ONE ENCHANTED EVENING

My cousin Goldie Cohen (Uncle Phil's daughter) lived next door to me when I was little, before we moved to James Avenue. She and my Aunt Evie, Mama's youngest sister, used to be my babysitters, in fact. Goldie and I were always very close so after she married Meyer Shubb, and moved with him and their two little girls to Sioux City Iowa I missed her.

I must have been about 21 or so when Goldie sent for me to come to Souix City for a New Years Eve party, she had a date for me, someone she wanted me to meet. Once I agreed to go, she also fixed Aunt Evie up as Aunt Evie was going to be my chaperone (in those days a young lady did not travel alone to a strange place. We went by bus or train, I don't recall which.) Aunt Evie was already married and divorced from her alcoholic husband.

My date was named Lou Chessin. His family invited Evie and me for dinner before the New Years Eve dance so they could look me over, I suppose. They were nice people and had a beautiful daughter who could neither speak nor hear. After dinner we went to the Club. As we ascended the circular staircase two attractive teenagers came bouncing down. "Hi, Popo, Hi Eppie," Lou greeted the Friedman twins, the future Abigail Van Buren and Ann Landers.

It was a nice evening but a fairly boring one for me. Sometime later, Lou came to Minneapolis with Goldie and Meyer and another couple so he could take me out. Goldie and Meyer sat in the front seat, the other couple in the back seat and I had to sit on Lou's lap in the back seat as well. He was a perfectly polite gentleman. We probably went to the Standard Club for dinner, I don't remember.

After that, Lou who was nearly thirty and well established in his fathers broom manufacturing business, came to take me out every few weeks, though I was not the least bit interested in him and was dating others inbetween. Why didn't I let him know I didn't have any interest? How could I insult my cousin's friend, and my cousin?

The following New Years Eve Mama, who thought Lou a great match for me, convinced me to invite Lou to my off-campus sorority party. As we walked into the Shedlov's living room, across the room by the Victrola, I saw a guy I'd never seen before. Little did I know that he was brought there by two of my girlfriends, Lakie and Bebel (both nicknames for Lillain which was the given name of both of them) who were his cousins. They had brought him to meet me, but not told me. They also wanted him to meet Maxine Levy, another eligible friend of theirs; though I doubt that they told her either.

We pulled names to see who would dance the first dance with whom and I drew his. So, I went over to the Victrola and showed Ralph Rossen that I'd drawn his name. "I'm not dancing," he replied, "My father died recently." So, we stood and talked for a while and then I went back and joined the rest of the party with whom I'd come.

I was really excited. He was a head taller than Lou Chessin, well built and strutting his figure, flexing his muscles and letting me know that he'd been a football player before Medical School. He had black hair and his blue eyes were just like my fathers.

On the way home, Lou proposed to me. He already had bought a ring, which my Mother had gone downtown Minneapolis to help him pick out. He offered me the ring. I was shocked and said, "No, thank you." He couldn't understand.

When I got into the house, Mama was waiting up for me. "Did anything exciting happen?" she asked anxiously. I couldn't even answer her I had to go to the bathroom so badly. So she followed me upstairs all the while asking "Did anything special happen?"

"Yes," I told her "something did. I met a really terrific guy. He's got a really terrific personality, he's so handsome and he's going to be a doctor."

"Is he in school?," she asked.

"Yes, he's a Junior in the Medical School," I told her. I thought she'd collapse she was so upset. He'd have years yet of training and I was getting on in age, and now her plans for my marriage to Lou had failed.

And poor Lou, later I wrote him a letter and said we'd been through a strange interlude and I apologized if I'd led him on. I had not intended to. I did not mention that I could not marry him because that very evening I'd met the man I wanted to marry.

Ralph didn't lose any time. He wanted to see me again but he had no money at all, so he needed another party. (He was working his way through school since his father had just died.) He got Lakie and Bebel to arrange one, and then he got his cousin Ralph Helstien to double date so we could use Ralph's car (Ralph Rossen didn't have one).

The party was at Bebel's. We had a very good time and had lots to talk about. He told me about the Range and how marvelous it was and how he wanted to become a Pediatrician and then go back and practice there as Pediatricians were so badly needed there.

above: Ralph Rossen, not yet M.D. circa: 1928

# 2. AN UNCONVENTIONAL WEDDING

Once Mama met Ralph she saw what I meant. She thought he was darling. But later on, everybody got involved in our business once it was clear that we were serious. We went together throughout the rest of Ralph's Medical Schooling, and through his internship and wanted to get married. But his Mother wanted him to take an offer from the CCC camps (125 dollars a month) and give it all to her since she was newly widowed, without money and still had two children, Ro and Manuel, at home. Besides she thought her girls, Minnie and Ro, should marry first.

But we didn't want to wait and Ralph did not want the CCC. He wanted to specialize. I agreed that he should have that chance; he was in demand in a couple of departments.

I knew and was good friends with Ralph's Aunt Rose, Lakie's mother (his mother's sister); she had been to our house for sorority teas. It was an offcampus sorority; a club, really of Minneapolis and St. Paul girls. But his Mother didn't like me, or at least the idea of me as she was opposed to his getting married at that point.

Meanwhile, my Mother was pressing for us to announce an engagement. She didn't want me to continue to be tied up with one person if it wasn't perfectly clear that we would marry. Too many people had their hands in my business. So I packed up and moved out, onto campus. I was independent by then; I'd gotten my $500 from Papa that he'd put away for me, and Papa got me started in a retail clothing business, a small women's shop on campus. It was on Oak Street near where the movie theater is now. My clientele was mostly nurses looking for dress clothes, and skirts and blouses. Papa was on my side all the time. He believed everybody should have a chance.

Below: a copy of my business card

1934 9 30

## BEA'S SMART SHOP

T DRESSES                         318 HARVARD S1
ART PRICES                        FENWICK AF

When Mama said we were engaged, my aunts all gave us china and crystal and stuff. But when I didn't appear excited enough, Aunt Lucy started messing and causing trouble. She said she thought we must already BE married. But she couldn't prove it, although she worked in Hennepin County Records Department. There was nothing there to show our marriage because we'd gone over to Hudson Wisconsin, gotten a Justice of the Peace and secretly eloped. It wasn't quite as easy as we thought it would be, though.

We thought we'd foiled everyone and it would easily remain a secret. We applied for the license and waited until it came. Then we went to the Justice's house, as per our appointment. But he said he needed witnesses. It so happened that his daughter and son-in-law were visiting. Would they be acceptable? Of course, we said, not having been able to supply our own witnesses for fear of their telling someone. But, lo and behold as his daughter rounded the staircase she yelled, "Ralph," she and her husband hugged and kissed him and then they all explained: they were all from Hibbing where she'd been one of his high school teachers. We then had to tell them of our plight and prevail upon them to keep our secret, which they apparently did.

But word got out. Aunt Lucy's instincts were correct and her detective work thorough. When she could not find any evidence of our marriage in Hennepin County Records, she began to search Wisconsin. Soon she had proof from Hudson, Wisconsin that Ralph and I were indeed married.

So Mama stopped worrying about announcing our engagement! His mother still did not know, though.

Above: Ralph Rossen, M.D., and his wife Beatrice Ruth Cohen
Rossen circa: 1937

# 3. AFTON

Ralph was specializing at the University in neurology. Not that it was his original plan. The plan was to return to Hibbing to practice Pediatrics. But, during the residency there was a polio epidemic in Duluth and they were bringing the kids down here. (The story was that the epidemic began in an open pickle barrel in a grocery store.) The only department at the University with any money to investigate polio and its origins, was neurology so he took his residency there.

Because they didn't pay at all nor supply board and room, he took a job at Shriner's Hospital which gave him board and room in exchange for Ralph doing their blood work early in the morning and sometimes late at night.

And that wasn't all. In order to have to give money to his mother and also to have some in his pocket he had a night practice in Afton, Minnesota. Minnie was teaching in the country and gave half her salary to her mother, Ro didn't drive, Manuel was in high school

I had my store on the campus and lived above it, or at home, when we first started going to Afton. They thought I was the doctor's nurse. We went there after we were married, too.

Every day after his residency, about five o'clock, Ralph and I went in our car to Afton, first getting our dinner—six hamburgers for a quarter at White Castle, a nickel for tea or pop and that supposedly was our dinner. (He had four hamburgers and I had two). Then we drove there in our $25 car—a Chrysler convertible. But then when we got to Afton Mrs. Reichert would have us in for a late supper. She was very nice about feeding us. She had some health problem and Ralph never charged her, he talked to her at home.

Our first office in Afton was two rooms upstairs of Gramma Penningtons Hotel. No electricity or running water in the building. (Nobody had any.) Mrs. Pennington taught me to clean and light the kerosene lamps and we went into the backyard and brought in a pail of water which we heated on a heating stove in the winter and used cold water in the summer. We needed it for Ralph to wash his hands, etc. The toilet was outside.

The second year we moved our office to the basement of the Post Office. We went every day. When we moved to the basement there was electricity and running water. Most of the people did not pay in cash because of the depression. If we picked up a dollar or two we were very surprised. Mostly they paid in eggs and chicken (live), which we took to St. Paul in the trunk in a crate to have kashered. That was how he got food for his mother—vegetables, eggs, chicken, etc.

Shriners had a wonderful garage and Ralph had a parking space and kept the chicken in the trunk there until he got them to the schochet.

One day a man who was grateful for the help Ralph and John Anderson were giving regarding his son who was very sick came with a gift for them. A tiny puppy. Ralph and John flipped a coin for him. Ralph won and John was relieved. We got a terrific friend. We named him Rufus. He lived at my mother's house, and stayed sometimes with Ralph at Shriners also. My folks often had dogs when we were growing up but his mother didn't like them. He and Lillian Gordon had a dog though, in Hibbing which they kept in the grocery store (which their fathers owned) and shared the chores of feeding him and taking him out.

# 4. ST. PETER STATE HOSPITAL

In 1935 Ralph's close friend, Herman Hilleboe, was already done with his residency. (He started the mobile unit to test for TB and then went national with it.) Ralph was on his residency, and Hermie asked Ralph if he would like a job in the State Hospital as long as he was training in neurology...he knew a man named Mr. Carlgren who was on the Board of Control and Mr. Carlgren had told Hermie that they were looking for someone to be Assistant Superintendent at the St. Peter State Hospital. The salary was $225 per month plus furnished apartment such as it was, plus a food allowance but not fruit and vegetables except in the summer when they grew on the farm.

We gave Ralph's mother $125 per month; he owed the University $500 for tuition which he borrowed after his father died. With the $100 that was left we had to start paying off that loan, pay our insurance, buy fruit and vegetables when they were not available, and we tried to have $5.00 per week as our allowance to do with as wanted or needed. I got my hair washed and set once a week...it cost 50 cents plus a dime tip; if we went to a show we each paid our own way, same with out to dinner.

I wanted to go to Gustavus because there was an outstanding man in speech named Anderson but they wouldn't let me go unless I took Religion but I didn't want religion. One of the women who worked in the cooking department saw to it that I could go up there and swim occasionally.

We had Rufus there. I was doing a lot of cooking because we were entertaining all the time. John and Albertine Anderson would come down from the U, Harry Loeb would come, and when they came they would spend a few days with us. I even made my own cottage cheese; they didn't have it at the hospital and it was too expensive downtown...Rufus loved it. (We could get milk at the hospital.)

Ralph was still going into the University one day a week. We had to go in and stay overnight—I stayed with my folks, he stayed at his Mothers or at the University. Ralph liked the patients at St. Peter but he wasn't happy about the patients that were in restraint, and took them out. He brought in the electric shock treatment program.

# 5. BIG CHANGES

In 1938 everything changed. You were born healthy on January 12, though I had a placenta previa and we both nearly died. We came home from the hospital two weeks later and stayed at my mother's so I could recuperate. Your father came every other day from St. Peter to visit us until we three went back to St. Peter.

Then, in April your father was named Superintendent of the Hastings State Hospital and we moved to Hastings. The previous superintendent had thirteen children so the house provided for us, on the grounds of the hospital was tremendous. You and your father always loved it, but I thought it was an old barn of a place. That became our home though for the next sixteen years except for the three years your father was in the Navy when we lived in Washington DC, Richmond and Norfolk, Virginia and the nearly two years he was Commissioner of Mental Health for the State of Minnesota, and we lived back on Upton and Plymouth.

Below: Superintendents residence on the grounds of the Hastings State Hospital, Hastings, Minnesota, which was our home for the better part of sixteen years.

# EPILOGUE

*By Arlene Rossen Cardozo*
*July, 2006*

If only Mother had lived to see Latvia and Lithuania, her parents' and grandparents' birthplaces, with Dick and me, our daughter Rebecca and her husband Chris in June 2001. Some weeks before our departure I contacted the Riga office of records and was assigned our Jewish genealogist, Rita, to whom I e-mailed all the information Mother had given us about her Grandma Fredrica's Feidelson family. What, if anything, after the Nazi era could possibly remain of our families' records?

Our historian guide Yulik, whose parents amazingly survived the Nazis, picked us up at the airport and took us directly to Rita who met us with such a big smile and large stack of papers that I burst out crying. We four were incredulous that she had found a tremendous amount of information. "You see," she explained, "the Nazis destroyed the people but kept all the records."

It turned out that fate, and fate alone kept us Feidelson/ Witebsky descendants alive, fruitful and multiplying through the generations while 41 others of our extended family (children and grandchildren of Fredrica Feitelson Witebsky's siblings) perished on one fateful morning in 1941 when the Nazis marched the Jews of Riga to the killing forest, gunned them down, and buried them in mass graves.

In Latvia, we found that we Feidelson descendants are indeed the remnant who remain, thanks to the forces that drove Adolph, Fredrica and their children from Riga at the beginning of the 1890s.

We visited Mitau, a small village about fifteen miles outside Riga where the Feidelsons had lived before moving to Riga. No Jews could live within the Riga city limits until the last half of the 19th century, thus the Jewish families lived in Mitau and the Jewish men were allowed to live in certain Riga men's houses during the week if their work was deemed important enough to the Riga economy. Eventually, through later correspondence and further genealogical work with Rita we traced the family back to before 1790 in Mitau. Since the Mitau Jews were known to have made their ways there from Germany, this bears out the story Mother had heard from Grandma Fredrica. Further, since many German Jews arrived in Germany sometime after the expulsions of all practicing Jews from Spain in 1492 and Portugal in the early 1500s, the story that the family was originally from Spain is historically likely.

We spent two days in Riga where we found the addresses, though there are no houses there now, of the Ber Moshe Feitelson and Minna Bernstein Feitelson family—(Grandma

Fredrica's parents)—and saw the lovely homes in which children and grandchildren of Grandma Fredrica's siblings lived before they were shot by the Nazis in 1941. We met people who knew family members, or who knew of them (again those people were from the very few who survived the Nazis). One woman who at age eleven had escaped with her parents to Siberia in 1940, remembered some of Grandma Fredrica's siblings and their children from the 1930s.

It was exhilarating to experience this part of our family history and to see the verdant green, green country and beautiful cultural city from which the family came. But all my years of learning about the Holocaust from university courses, my own academic research, meeting with hundreds of direct Holocaust survivors, some of the concentration camp liberators, visiting Yad Vashem and other major Holocaust museums throughout the world, did not bring home what these two days in Riga did. It made me realize that we are indeed the remnant, and absent the Nazi era, where six million European Jews were brutally murdered (among them forty-one of our extended family members) our trip to Riga would have been very different. We might have stayed for days and days eating in their homes and exchanging family stories with hundreds of our Feidelson cousins.

But, as all survivors learn: life goes on. And we, the remnant who remain of the Feitelson family and who returned to Riga, went out to dinner and celebrated that, once again from Pharaoh to Hitler, those who hate we Jews have failed to extinguish us.

978-0-595-40671-5
0-595-40671-8

Printed in the United States
121356LV00004B/70-87/A